All The Things I Shouldn't Have Said

Ragan Oliver

BookLeaf Publishing

India | USA | UK

Presentation by *BookLeaf Publishing*

Web: www.bookleafpub.com

E-mail: info@bookleafpub.com

ISBN: 9789358317299

First edition 2023

DEDICATION

To every version of myself who never thought I'd survive to see another day. The cats still need to be fed tomorrow.

ACKNOWLEDGEMENT

This whole thing would have never been possible without so many people in my corner and out of it.
Revan, thank you for being my best work of art.
Blue, thank you for being my first commenter.
Courtney, thank you for always answering the call.
Katherine, thank you for always keeping me real.
To everyone I've ever loved, thank you for being my muse.
To everyone who has ever broken my heart, thank you for being my muse.

PREFACE

Here they are: a collection of words that probably shouldn't have been published. But they were. Some of these words were written with specific people in mind. Some of them were written for myself. The majority of them were written in response to a state of mind. But all of them were written with the intention to allow you to feel less alone. Because you're not alone. You are never alone.

The Thing

I did that thing again.
The thing where I strike the match and watch it
burn.
The thing where I say some shit that makes you
hurt.
The thing where I get lost in the sauce of my
insecurities and drunk off of the idea that no one
as great as you could ever love someone as
broken and fucked up as me.
The thing where I run my mouth and ask too
many questions and I give too many answers
and I project my insecurities onto you to paint
you into the broken masterpiece of my own
demise.

I did that thing again.
The thing where I should have just walked away.
The thing where I should have just listened to
what you had to say.
The thing where I should have just allowed you
to speak and thanked you for speaking directly
to me.
The thing where I should have just recognized a
boundary and stopped in my tracks but instead, I
kept pushing forward without ever looking back.

I did that thing again.
That thing where I burned it all to the ground in
hopes to light a fire bright enough to keep me
warm in my bed all alone.

But it never works because it will eventually
burn out.
And I'll be left with the charred remains of what
could have been but was never meant to be.

Again

You once wrote the words:
'We're just distant stars, orbiting in opposite
directions.'
I wish that was the case for you and I
Because then at least I'd be on your mind.
Because god knows I can't get you out of mine.

So I drew my lines in the sand
Of this fragile fucking wasteland
And with these bruises and broken hands
I pull out my heart and write you one last
request:
Will you please give me another chance?

But I know that you won't ever read it, or really
stop for recollection.
Because in the next line you wrote:
"But when we pass each other, this time we
don't crash with affection."
And to crash would require of our paths an
intersection.
But god also knows that I was only made for
rejection.

Cottagecore

My name is the song I want you to sing between
your breaths.
The resounding sound of my heartbeat crashing
through my chest.
The shattering of my rib cage as I crack it wide
to rip out my heart.

A wedding gift from me to you.
A reminder that my life is in your hands.

You're the most beautiful art I've ever seen.
You could be hanging in a museum or painted on
the ceiling.

Like the feeling of your bedroom after the one
night I spent with you.
Waking up with our clothes still on as the light
from the sun came crashing through.

As your dog came crashing through.

As my feelings came crashing through.

As I watched you breathe in your sleep and felt
your heartbeat against mine.

And I thought "Jesus Christ that's the most
beautiful tempo I've ever matched."

As I traced crooked lines across your skin.
And I thought "Jesus Christ I could line the
insides of my brain with this feeling and never
need another antidepressant again."

Connecting the freckles on your shoulders,
drawing roadmap to the arteries in your neck.
The interstate highway to your heartbeat.

That I wanted nothing more than to beat for me.

To provide the rhythm for my next love poem.

Tie the string so I could never get lost.

The compass rose of your smile as the crosshairs
in the scope of the rifle used to murder my
doubt.

I wanted to murder your doubt.

To make you believe in fairytales.

Make you believe in love at first sight.

To make you believe that you're beautiful.

Because you are.

To put a ring made of string on your finger and run the line from your hand to mine just so I could look at you in a room full of people and say in my best southern drawl "wow what a catch".

To run the line from your finger to mine and tug on the strings of time.
While they pluck out the soundtrack of our life.

Of 20 years before we had our first fight.

Of 20 years of me waking up before daylight to make you coffee.

Of 20 years of you stealing the blankets off of me in our cabin in the woods that you keep so cold that only the heat of our bodies and the fire in our love ever keep me warm.

Left Turn

It's crazy how one, solitary circumstance in a
complete, continuous register of conditions and
happenings can change the entire trajectory of a
journey.

A single wrong turn...
The smallest shift of a compass...
A misprint in the directions...
The tiniest of misunderstandings.

No matter the magnitude.

No matter how miniscule it seems from the
start...

Or how infinite the gravity of an...
Individual...
Independent...
Autonomous...
Conversation may appear.

No matter how unaffected you may feel by...
The slightest shift in mood...
Or change of temperature...
Or misalignment of the stars.

It only takes the faintest of faults for the planet
to leave the Goldilocks Zone and become a
completely inhospitable wasteland.

And why should we be any different?

I've spent my entire life...
Walking on eggshells...
Waiting for the coming cataclysm...
The following flux...

The sequential superabundance of shambles that
would shake me to my core and devastate me for
the rest of my life.

I've spent so many of my days dodging
doomsday after disarray after disaster.

It's become an art form...
The waltz of weary feet...
Reminiscent of the broken glass...
Spiteful screams from the downstairs kitchen...
While I curled up in the attic floor...
Surrounded by the dirty diapers...
And circus peanut candies that...
I had grown accustomed to hiding.

It's incredible how quickly you can learn the
steps of the dance...
and the lines to the script of survival when your
life depends on it.

And what's even more incredible is...
How long it takes you to forget the script...
The supporting roles...
That you've been cast to play...
Become ingrained in your DNA.

Never in the spotlight...
Never wanting to be the center of attention...
Craving only to exist in the background...
Never making your presence known...
For fear of what would happen if your name...
Was to be included in the...

Ending credits.

Carried forward by stage fright...
The lines etched into your brain...
Like the carving on the gravestone of your
youth...
Withered by age and the elements...
Sometimes illegible and unrecognizable...
But never truly gone.

Never truly forgotten.

Never truly erased.

Always buried six feet deep in your brain.

In your personality.

In your soul.

Locked away in a tomb of suppressed memories
and trauma responses.

The hint of horror that causes your heart to stop
for a brief moment when someone raises their
voice at you.

The tremble of terror that escapes your pores
when his hand grazes your skin on accident and
in passing.

The particle of panic that catches in your throat
when your brain reminds you that you're
always...

The second choice...

The never good enough...

The afterthought...

The disillusioned...
Disappointment...
Of a daughter.

The prodigal child who never came back.

The inconvenience...
The selfish...
The broken...
The histrionic...
The problem...

But it was only when I stepped out of that
comfort zone...
When I rewrote the narrative...
When I became selfish...
When I turned right instead of left...
When I made the active decision to defend
myself...
And to recognize my worth...
And to honor and advocate for that child
quivering on the stairs in that...
Cold...
Lonely...
Loud...
Vermont apartment...

When I chose myself for once...

That's when I found you.

And I'd be lying if I tried to even pretend like it
doesn't scare the absolute shit out of me.

I can't even masquerade as if I'm unaffected by
the sight of your face on my phone screen...
or like my heart doesn't skip a beat every single
time your name comes up in conversation.

Because I know that offering you anything more
than the bare minimum means that I'm offering
you the ability to completely annihilate and
obliterate me—
and I don't have very many respawns and
rebuilds left to my name.

But I also know that offering you anything less
than absolutely all of me is wholly and
undoubtedly out of the question.

You see, behind that smile...
Under the cynicism and derision...
Cloaked in the façade of fixed and unwavering
fortitude...
hides a small child much like me.

Frightened...

Weary...
Anxious...
Hungry...

Craving a commodity that she has come to
conclude is claimed for everyone but her.

All she wants is to be enough...
Good enough...
Smart enough...
Pretty enough...
Nice enough...
Loveable enough.

Loveable enough to be...

Loved.

All you want is to be loved.

And all I want is to love you.

So here I am...
Alone in this apartment overlooking a city that I
have called home for over two thirds of my
life...
Pretending to be a tourist for a change of scenery
and a change of pace...

thinking about the number of ways that I can
allow you to change my plans.

Because it only took one left turn for me to lose
myself into the silent streets of the city that I
should know like the back of my hand...
but yet it only took you smiling at me from
across the sidewalk when you introduced
yourself to me for the first time for me to realize
that I was lost in you.

This is for you.

And you deserve so much more.

J.T.J.M.

Elbert Hubbard once said "Secrets are things we give to others to keep for us..." However true, however false, I have something I need to tell you now. I have not been completely honest with you to date...

In fact, there are many things about me that you would not know by simply coming in passing. Like the color of my blood as it was shed for this life or the anthem songs that wrote the lyrics of my strife.

This is not another sappy love poem. This is not another cliché in which I say with the words of my mouth that you kiss so softly, then say "it's just not working, ok?"

This is an uprising. This is a revolt in the purest of senses. An upheaval of all that you know and all that you hold and all that love has taught you so. As the thunder rolls in and the tide rolls out I'll throw your body into the waves and use you as bait to lure in another defenseless love who is star-stricken by the idea that I could be "the one".

Did you enjoy our first meeting or leave feeling like I stole your soul? Because I left that coffee shop wondering how long it would be before everything that I knew and everything I was would be sold. Sing your song before we're too far gone and nothing can be done because I really wonder if I'm really someone that you wanted to get to know or am I someone you just wanted to fuck?

I swear to god there's more days than not that god isn't real these days and some days when I look in the mirror I don't see a reflection of a creator just the broken pieces of my own damned and ugly face, but you continue to call that beautiful one moment then spit on it the next. It's the carousel of our love... just hate and sex. I can't keep up with your athletic, artistic whiplash bullshit anymore. I can't be the anthem song of all the things that you hate to adore. I can't be the one who just sucks it up and chokes it down and grins and bears it without making a sound.

You see, artists are pointless without the muse. Photographers without pictures are like poets without words- just human beings with nothing to offer the world and so I have to wonder if this is you or if you're here for a purpose. Was I just the game? The thrill? The hunt? Or the prize at the bottom of the stale, sugary cereal box that you really never planned to enjoy? Was I just another toy? An item to entertained for a moment before being discarded to the bottom of a bin or sold at a yardsale when you needed more room or you were moving on? Are you moving on?

I'm not really sure, but I can tell you that I do know that your photoshopped guitar pictures that you think look artistic and hipster are actually cocky, arrogant, and conceded as fuck. And I can tell you that I do know that you weren't really all that great of a fuck. And I can tell you that I do know that your mother loved me, and my friends hated you, and honestly, I never needed you like you never needed me.

I never needed you like you never needed me.

Damaged Goods

Just to note, my "preexisting condition" exists only because the conditions of the existence of men who caused them. The conditions of their souls, their conscious, is what created my "preexisting condition", what caused me sleepless nights at the hands of every settling of my walls, each creak a reminder of the mattresses that told my story, every word written into the stitching across the fabrics of my waking nightmares in cold sweats and cut up forearms- the stitching matching hospital visits and fluorescent tube lights, buzzing sounds inside the halls of Fort Sanders and inside the walls of my brain like a thousand angry hornets, each tearing at my insides with butcher knives shaped like words like "this is how daddies love their daughters" and "if you hadn't drank so much then this would be harder" and "you're supposed to love me. Why don't you love me?".

Their voices are charred into the walls of my memories, family photos and formal portraits a burning reminder of the fragility of the straw house protecting my mind from the elements. Each syllable a tsunami, the sound of their

alcohol slurred voices receding into the depths
of my subconscious, wreaking havoc on my
fundamental definition of self before a tidal
wave of reminders barrels towards the shore, the
sights, the smells, the feeling of his hands on my
knee and his fingers on my shoulder and his lips
on my ears.

Oh my God, I was a child.
I was a freshman.
I was your girlfriend.

I am not a victim, but a perpetrator painted
through perverted words like alcoholic,
tease,
addict,
bitch,
cunt,
slut,
whore.

I wanted it, don't you know? That's why I fought
tooth and nail to escape until I had exhausted all
of my resources.
Exhausted my energy.
Exhausted my will.
My will to escape.
My will to recover.
My will to live.

A Stockholm Syndrome with my own
depression,
An alliance carved in the flesh of my own life,
road lines and street signs etched into forearms
and thighs that mapped the routes in which you
traveled. Your conquest a manifest destiny of
irrevocable justification.

If I only made you love me less.
If I only drank less.
If I only loved you better.
It was after all your divine right to conquer new,
uncharted territory. It was in your nature to fight
for what you can't have.
The struggle made it all worth it.

All words that slip into the dreams of every
survivor, flipping the script and changing the
dialogue to paint the skies with dark blacks and
blues, the colors that lines our wrists and
elbows, bruises to tell stories that fade into
nothing but a memory, a nightmare, a mistyped
and misrepresented memorial of who we once
were.

A reminder of the damages done.

A Crack in the foundation of my sanity, allowing
darkness to seep through with every cold breeze.

With every cut mark that lined my wrists a little
more entered through the hustle and bustle of the
blood trying to escape- business men in passing,
struggling through the rush hour traffic of the
subway station of my mind. Every train car
screeching behind schedule with voices shouting
"no" and "please don't" just moments, days,
weeks too late.

Recovery looked like a missed train, waiting on
the darkened station for the next one. Anxiety
filled eyes darting to and from every
corner-stander and passers-by.

Recovery looked like countless failed sexual
encounters that ended in tears streaming like
water faucets designed to drown myself in my
own despair.

It was sitting in a doctor's office waiting room to
hear "well, what were you wearing?" and
knowing the irony of the fact that I would never
feel safe in a suicide prevention shirt ever again.

From the day I was born, that day in 1994, 2008,
2010, I have never been safe, fighting a war

against myself and against others like him, stretching my resources too far, too thin across the board, the veil thinning until it tears, ripping at the seams that hold me together, my heavy limbs falling to the floor with a crash only rivaled by that of a nuclear explosion.

But I am a mother fucking phoenix, bursting into flames and burning this shit to the ground.

You can not escape the empirical proof of the existential remains of my fallout.

You see, nuclear fallout steadily fades and can be avoided. You can recover through disposing of your clothes and showering-ironic saying that those are the two things that we are taught to avoid as survivors.

But I couldn't stand the idea of your sweat on my skin, dancing across my pores any longer than the minutes that you whispered those words, "if you scream, I'll kill your sister", "Shut up and bend the fuck over", and "this is what you're supposed to do."

But you cannot escape this.

Knowing that potentially with every news article
and every Facebook post that scrolls across your
feed, you are reminded of the monster that lives
behind your crooked smile fuels my fires and
feeds the explosion.

Knowing that you will see my face painted
across banners and news broadcasts, every
picket line and every protestor a representation
of the atomic blast that you only began to create.

See, if you play with fire, you will be burned
and honey, I am a matchbook in hell.
The only thing hotter than this desire to watch
you crumble is my desire to lift others up from
the ashes.

And you see, fire only becomes stronger the
larger the blaze gets so watch us burn as we burn
this mother fucking shit to the ground.

You see, my "preexisting condition" is only
preexisting because of the condition of someone
else's existence... a group of someones who will
remain unharmed and unaffected by Healthcare
changes and political by-laws... but me, my
Healthcare is in danger simply because of the
sick, fucked up condition of rapists and sexual
predators like a specific walking, talking

OompaLoompa with a short man complex and a
terrible toupee...

My "preexisting condition" speaks more about
the condition of the men who wounded me than
it ever will about me- about my life. About my
character.
My "preexisting condition" tells the story of a
survivor. Not a victim, but a victor.

And just like the men and women before me, the
Warriors of truth and survival, I will not go
gently.

We will not go silently.

We will not go calmly.

And just like every day since 1994, since 2008,
and since 2010, I will fight for my life.

I will fight for your life.

And I will fight for the life of every survivor.

Because I am not damaged goods.

And I will not go down without a fight.

And #IAmNotAPreexistingCondition

A letter to my friend pondering suicide:

Dear friend pondering suicide,

Yes, I want to kill myself too. Don't worry though, this won't happen. I'm not actively planning my demise. I'm not consciously thinking of all of the ways that I could go out. I'm not sculpting my suicide letter as we speak. But I do want to kill myself.

You see, this is the tricky thing about my depression—It's sort of always there. In fact, thinking back, I can't ever really recall a time that it wasn't there. I mean, I've had a great life. I've had a fucked up, shitty life, but in spite of it all, I've had a great life. I was fostered by 2 of the greatest human beings that have ever walked this earth. I've had a plethora of great friends who were there when I needed them. I have a few amazingly perfect friends who are still around through it all. I have some amazing memories and fun times that I will always be able to reflect on—but even when I look back on these great times, depression is there.

The third grade was a great time of learning and exploration for me. I had a great teacher who invested time in my interests and helped foster a love of learning in my little mind. Third grade was also the year that I cried almost every morning when I woke up because I didn't want to go to school because I thought I wasn't going to be good enough to make my grandparents happy and they were going to "send me back". The sixth grade was an amazing year for my writing. I met a teacher who encouraged me to write, even if I had no clue how to form a sentence or how to engage an audience (be patient—I'm still learning). She told me to just write, reading every shitty story about fighting robots and elves that I managed to pump out on notebook paper held together by paperclips and half-assed attempts at stapling jobs. This was also the year where I became convinced that I was too overweight to be a cheerleader when all of my friends where trying out—and I allowed myself to become angry at them for it. In seventh grade, I got my first degree black belt. This was an amazing dream come true, but this was also the year that I cried myself to sleep every night because I was "sad but I can't explain why." In senior year of high school, everything was lining up perfectly for me. I had the best best friend that I could ever ask for (who has still stuck with me in spite of being dragged through the pits of depression, addiction, suicide, anger, sadness, and every other human emotion and character defect that you could imagine). I had an amazing boyfriend who genuinely cared. I had scholarships to college and was a star athlete, and battalion commander in ROTC, and competing in marketing international competitions, and language festivals, and going to skate parks and concerts every weekend, and competing in karate tournaments, and loving the life that I was living to the fullest, and still hyperventilating on my drives home and locking myself inside of my bathroom with razor blades and lighters.

Depression is like that person who invites themselves to everything you do—even when you don't want them there. Depression is that family member who always manages to remind you that one of your cousins is doing something slightly better than you. Depression is that one dark cloud in the sky, letting you know that even if it is bright and shining where you are, somewhere, out there, it is raining.

Do you remember those commercials from when you were growing up where they were marketing depression as a bathrobe or a dark cloud following you? I always laughed at these because, as I understood it, depression wasn't anything like that. You see, for the longest time, I didn't think that I had depression. I didn't think that depression could be progressive. I didn't think that alcoholism could be progressive. I didn't think that addiction and suicide and pain of the brain and the heart could be progressive. No, depression was something that was always there, making it impossible to move. Pain was crippling and debilitating. So to have this little blue bathrobe following you, draping itself over your shoulders while you're still able to walk through your neighborhood to work—that was impossible. People died from this disease—they didn't function like I do.

But I came to realize, slowly and painfully, that this wasn't true. It took years for me to understand why when I was sitting with friends at dinner, having the time of my life, I could be joking and laughing until stomach hurt and then in the very next breath, I could be overwhelmed with a desire for a car to run through the three-way intersection and crash into the building right outside my window, killing me instantly. It took me a long time to realize that not everyone thinks about turning their steering wheel suddenly to the left into oncoming traffic or googles what the chances are of being struck by lightning. You see, that, my friends, is my depression. It isn't always being unable to get out of bed. It isn't always being incapable of going to work or being productive or getting things done. It isn't always an overwhelming desire to end my life or anything. My depression is a constant lingering feeling of "well, this is fun, but do you know what else would be fun? Dying."

That's not to say that your depression, no matter how similar or how different, isn't real. No, friends, your depression is very, very real. But even more so than your depression, so are you. You are real, and you are strong, and you are brave—even if you don't feel it. Underneath that cloud and underneath that bathrobe and underneath that overwhelming boulder, or sheet, or veil, or sad song, or behind those sweat covered trembling hands, there is a real, strong, powerful, brave, beautiful human being who is breathing, feeling, and living—and some days that is enough.

You are enough.

You shouldn't have had to be enough. You shouldn't have had to be strong. But you were. And you are. And I'm thankful for that.

Place your hand on your chest. I know it's silly, but humor me. Skin to skin, palm on your chest. Do you feel that warmth? It may be faint, but the average temperature of a human body is 98.6 and the proteins in a human body begin to degrade at 106 degrees. So the reality is that we're always just degrees away from being too hot to handle, and I hope that makes you smile enough to remember that I love you.

I may want to kill myself. You may want to kill yourself. But we are alive. We are here. And I am proud of you for that. And even if you don't hear it any more today, hear it now. You are enough.

I am proud of you.

With love,
A friend pondering suicide.

It's Nice to Finally Meet You

Hi.

It's nice to finally meet you.

The sounds of the bar patrons and the local band have finally died down and it's just you and me and the moon tonight. The trees stand guard as you breathe into the darkness the smoke that exits your lungs, waltzing into the crisp air that has wrapped itself tightly around you. How I crave to be wrapped tightly around you—to hold your body at its most vulnerable peaks, to tiptoe across the goosebumps that mark the constellations across your skin, mapping the lines of the cosmos from the beginning to end—start to finish. Start. To finish. How I long to see your finish. To taste your finish. To feel your finish wrapping tightly across my fingers until your body gives out and you collapse on the…

What was that?

Oh, nothing… I'm just thinking about the moon again. Isn't it interesting how it phases in and out… waxing and waning… appearing closer and closer… so close you can almost touch it… feel it… caress it… I'll pretend to be thinking about the phases of the moon while attempting to pretend that I'm not phased by you… The blue rimmed glasses have done little to protect me from falling into the labyrinth of your eyes. The twists and turns of topaz and sienna wrapped tightly in the vivid views of intoxicating landscapes and deep forests of jade green that contrast against the darkened pine that holds it all in tightly. You're a goddamned Bob Ross painting and us meeting can't be anything better than a happy little accident… The dark eyeliner that traces around your eyelids… it provides the perfect frame to the perfect artwork of your gaze… your skin… the innumerable freckles that trace cosmic creations across the bridge of your nose and your forehead Ombre outward arriving at the edges of your face with the slightest, lightest of tones.

Your body… THAT BODY… that moves in perfect rhythm with mine… a symphony of motion like waves in the ocean. I want to drown between your thighs. Please write my mother… I'm a sailor lost at sea… that perfect body that fits so perfectly with mine… I told you, honey, stretch marks are fine—after all, I learned when

I was younger how to color between the lines…
My lips connecting the dots between freckles
and beauty marks, the constellations drawn by
the hand of god herself that write the story of
creation. The Big Bang. The climax of where we
take this situationship to a relationship. I want
you to wake up in the morning wondering why
you feel so hungover until an hour into your
workday when you're suddenly dripping wet
remembering the way that your body hung over
the side of the couch. I wonder if that stain on
your cushion ever came out?

I want you to taste the words on my tongue—the
marriage of sweetness like honey and smokiness
of nicotine that lingers on your likes has me
hearing wedding bells for this kiss… Dearly
Beloved, we are gathered here together in the
sight of god, our moon—and in the face of this
company of just you and me and the sheets that
line your bed. I'd put on music, but I'm afraid
I'll miss a single sound that exits your mouth…

Oh… speaking of god, I want to enter into your
cathedral, kneel down at your alter and open the
hymnal of songs that you have memorized verse
for verse and I want to hear you scream… I
mean, sing. As your living room becomes my
new chapel where prayers to god are answered.

I've never seen the face of Jesus so clearly as when I swear to god you stopped my heart. I'm not talking about the white Jesus that I grew up with. No. This had to be the same Holy Spirt that I saw when my friend took me to his church where women were passing out and fanning themselves because being in the presence of absolute perfection was almost too much to handle and their voices that cried out sounded like speaking in tongues… and let me tell you baby, I may not be fluent in a foreign language anymore, but that Duo Lingo Owl hasn't sent me a push notification in a while, so let me show you what this tongue can do. Let me speak the language of your mind… of your body… of your…

What?

Oh, sorry.

I just got distracted for a moment…

 It's just really nice out…

The moon is…

Pretty.

I'm Ragan.

It's nice to meet you.

Places

Your cries are ripped out from your charred lungs- crashing with art still on your bedroom sky. I'm holding you, my voice still with a shaky tongue- in the bedroom where I heard you take back your life. You swore to me your life just ended the moment that he broke off his cold embrace. You said this unfamiliar world was suspended in a special time that couldn't be replaced. We can't carry on with our disguise.

The snow burned from under our noses on the black tar paths with broken street lights. I wonder if you thought you'd still feel this hopeless if we ever made it out of here alive. I pondered how hard it would be to live a life worth ending- shaking through shallow breaths and the sweating embrace. My unfamiliar world this powder blended with the terror of the demons with my own face. I can't keep hiding behind this disguise.

His scent still echoes like a knife- surgery on the grey parts I can't see. I trusted him with my life, but that's exactly what he took from me. If I've learned anything from this room with you, it's

that living can be the hardest thing we can do.
You're too good for this world but it won't be
the same without you. I don't want to wake up
tomorrow and hear that your life has ended. I
don't want black dresses and your brother's
embrace. It's this unfamiliar house that we have
rented. This isn't you, it's this dreaded place.

Sinking, Drowning, and the Definition of Swimming

Do you know what it feels like to be sinking?

It felt like being god's best work and the Devils best friend, kissing Blunts and liquor bottles just to fill the void of her on my lips.

Eating drugs like candy, I was A kid released in Willy Wonka's factory, chewing the gum of addiction in spite all of the warning from McGruff the crime dog and every D.A.R.E. class that the 90s could produce.

Yes, I bloated like a balloon, swollen knuckles and angry veins, and floated my way to the ceiling, the hiccups of momentary sobriety being the only thing to bring me back down to the real world.

You told me that my love was your drug and you prayed for an overdose, but really there was no room in your veins for the smack that you talked, so it flooded into mine and I opened the dams, allowing the chemicals to flow through my system, the virus to shut down my

computers, the faculties that told me that you
were bad for me.

You see, you were toxic waste and my hazmat
suit had a hole in the gloves where you had
burned through every time I held back your hair
while you threw up more lies about how I was
yours.

I mean, I only wanted you to love me like you
loved her and you loved Miss Molly more than
you loved yourself, but the problem is that your
heart wasn't big enough for two women and you
chose the drugs over me.

But I don't blame you because after you returned
my house key, I chose the drugs over locking my
doors and I allowed everyone to walk in,
bringing their friends with them.

You see, Charlie brought Dimitri, his friend from
South America, and my Georgia Home Boy
made sure that I slept softly that night. My
friend Hannah and her Aunt Mary woke me up
with some Special K, and I'm not talking about
cereal. Adam, Molly, and Clarity took me to
raves, while Tina made sure I never had to sleep
again.

You see, sleeping brought dreams and dreams turned to nightmares and nightmares turned to you and that's when I turned to drugs- because creating my own hell was easier than living in the sloppy seconds you left behind, the names of women and lovers who I had never even met before I met you. I learned the names of drugs like I knew the names of bands from the early 2000s, and by god, I could win Jeopardy based around the pop-punk revolution alone.

I never thought that I would be laying in my bed at 330pm, 6 years after the last time that I heard your voice apologize empty words like empty syringes, my lips tingling with the words I never found myself sober enough to speak you.

They say that it takes 7 years for your body to completely regenerate every cell inside of it, and I cannot wait for the day that there isn't a single cell of mine that you have touched, but the problem is that while cells regenerate, scars never heal and the lines that you left on my wrists, and in my brain can never flood out the lines in my veins and while it's been almost 6 years since I last picked up, I find myself still licking my lips when the nurse draws my blood.

Back then, even sending you a text message left
me stuck between "I don't wanna fuck this up"
and "I wanna get fucked up" so I just decided to
drink until the bottle was emptier than I felt-
which in case you wanted to know, the Atacama
Desert gets less than 1 millimeter of rain in a
year, but even with this, life manages to continue
in the Atacama, which is more than could be
said about me.

You see, when you walked out on me, you forgot
to close the door and hate wandered in, choking
out every ounce of self-consideration that I
could have even produced.

You left behind your addictions, suffocating me
with their hands around my neck, grip tightening
and trembling like my fingers every time that I
held that needle or hallowed out pen.

The ink drained out to write the words "I. Am.
Ok. " over and over again like a detention school
writing assignment designed to convince me of
the words that I lied daily for months after you
left.

Still now they leave a bitter taste in my mouth,
burning a scar on my tongue to match my wrists,
the anthem of my liar's curse.

I am OK.

I am OK.

I am OK.

I swear to god I am OK.

Phrases repeated over and over again, like a
siren song stuck on repeat.

This is the last time.

This is the last time.

This is the last time.

And it's always the last time.

But it'll never be the last time.

Because I have tried making it stop.

I have tried turning it off and back on again.

I have tried blowing in the cartridge.

I have tried unplugging it and plugging it back in again, but somehow drowning in a bottle seemed easier than drowning in my own mind and as long as I was under the waterline, I knew that I couldn't see your face.

But it wasn't until someone pulled me out of the water and into their boat that I realized what floating really felt like.

And it wasn't until her lips touched mine that I realized the difference in rescue breaths and suffocation.

And it wasn't until she saved me that I realized that the reason you were so eager to throw me overboard was because your ship was sinking anyway and that sacrificing me would lighten your load.

So I don't blame you.

I mean, it was me who forgot how to swim.

But I wish you the best at the bottom of the sea.

Sticks and Stones

It's time to drop the mortar baby
Bombs to light up the fucking sky
Make me a goddamned martyr honey
For this cause I would gladly die
I will leave this city in disorder
The symptoms of the public outcry
Sink every ship in the fucking harbor
Fide the down as I wave goodbye
Don't forget I'm the revolution starter
I signed up for this sinner's life
I'll meet you in the devil's parlor
For my crimes I will be crucified

Fuck
I don't think I'm quite ready to die
but I will if there's no way to make it home alive

You never thought I'd make it on my own
You can't trust me when I'm left alone
The blood you spilled to craft this warzone
Left me carving out my own gravestone
I never thought it would be so well-known
That you clearly have no backbone
So sit your ass on the fucking throne
As the kings and queens of sticks and stones

You're the king of stick and stones

There's only one thing left to say
And that's
Leave
Me
Alone
No
Why can't you just move on

You never thought I'd make it on my own
When only darkness was left to show
And you left with no other place to go
Now you're the one without a home
You fucked up when your fist met with my
jawbone
And when you convinced me of too much skin
and bones
Goddamn it must hurt to be overthrown
As the kings and queens of sticks and stones

I need to you listen to the sound of my voice
Because I will not be saying this again

You're the king of stick and stones

Sunken Ships

All systems are failing. I'm stuck below. All this ice and cold. My words mean nothing. But they're still shouted. Through my teeth as they chatter. Break my heart. Make me shatter. Watch my life. As it falls apart. Remind me of the hours. When we stood like giants. Our arms outstretched. Fighting the horizon. Sinking towards the west. This place won't ever be. Anything more than. What it seems. And everything. Will always be. Nothing more than. Courage to scream. Don't talk of life or love. Or ask me about what it means. To keep my head above. Shouting out. In one final plea. "Bury me. At the bottom of the sea". At least I'll be at home. With other treasure chests. Filled with wasted opportunity. There's so much more. This is just the start. My hands keep shaking. So you'll have to stitch up. These broken hearts.

The Bowling Ball, The Albatross, and Keanu Reeves

85 miles per hour is a standard of life for me these days. It's like that movie with the bus where if the speedometer got under a certain gage marker, everyone on board would die.
What was the name again?
Oh yeah.
Speed.
Funny how that works isn't it? I mean I could never get myself to go fast enough… isn't that why we pumped the chemical into our veins? I mean if we filled ourselves from the inside out surely our insides would be able to catch up with the world outside of us right? But it was never enough was it?
I mean do we honestly believe that Keanu Reeves was driving that fast enough to make that jump from one Interstate cliff to the next? Do we honestly believe that a bus that heavy ,filled with that many people, would have cleared the distance to safety? I mean no matter how much gas he gave it, no matter how much poison filled my lungs, no matter how much alcohol filled my blood, it was never enough to slow the chaos that ensued around me.

It was never enough to catch up.
And so it was easier to just bring everything to a screeching halt. with one swift movement horizontally across my forearms, stretched out from one corner to the next filling the void, or rather creating it, an opening from which all of the darkness inside, all of the speed, all of the liquor, all of you…. could leave.
And I could finally be empty.
I could finally be
Hollow.
I could finally be light enough to clear the distance from this world to the next, to make that jump. And that is all it took. With a bite of my lip and one quick turn of the steering wheel, I attempted the jump that physics alone has proved Keanu Reeves could not make, no matter how much Sandra Bullock was encouraging him. No matter how fast the bus was going. No matter how light or how hollow or how bled dry it was.
I was.
Do you know that the average school bus weighs 19 thousand pounds?
Do you know that the average school bus weighs 19k thousand pounds and a competition grade women's bowling ball weighs on average 12 pounds and right now my body is somewhere in between a bus filled with an entire Bowling

team, and I am sinking. Hurdling towards the end of a construction zone with both feet on the gas. I know how this ends.

I've seen that YouTube video where the pretentious physicist explains how Sandra and Kenna would have just killed everyone on board, but what if that was my point? What if I wanted to die?

Because every single night since I can remember, I've laid my head down to the anthem song of the darkness screaming into my ear "you fucked up again".

I mean, that's what it's like, isn't it? Living with a disorder? It's like a 19 thousand pound bus or a bowling ball strapped to my chest suffocating the air from my lungs and somehow through all of the terror that I experience, through all of the adrenaline, and all of the fight or flight, I manage to still find happiness in this, or at least the illusion of such. I mean can you ever be happy with an albatross hanging around your neck?

Coleridge wrote that poem about a sailor who shot a helpless bird and was forced to wear it is punishment, but the only thing that I have managed to shoot is more speed through my veins and liquor out of plastic glasses. I'm not sure how this works. I'm not sure how it is the same, but apparently it is, or else I would not be sinking.

So fuck you Coleridge. And fuck you Keanu reeves. And fuck you Sandra Bullock and fuck you to every person who ever told me to "cheer up" or "smile and you'll feel better" or to "just get over it," because my addiction and my illness wasn't visible enough to call in a sick day for.

Because why call in sick when your brain has raped, pillaged, and plundered every bit of happiness from your existence and it is taking everything in you to not walk in front of traffic or walk off of the side of the world?

I'm sorry that my illness wasn't visible enough to for you but maybe if your dress code didn't require long sleeves you could catch a glimpse of the war zone that is being painted on my insides.

Maybe if your workplace violence policy incorporated sexual harassment in its definition of violence instead of "water cooler banter" and "Why can't you take a joke" then you would be able to see the bruises scarred into the subconscious of my wrists as I relive the trauma of my assault with every "it was just a joke" and "god you're so uptight…"

And maybe if your absence policy worked around my mental health, you could see the

hurricane building in my insides, ten thousand
butterflies with razor blade wings fluttering
through my chest, demolishing the coastline that
once harbored the ship of my soul, a frigate that
is battered and worn, but still afloat in spite of
the rough seas it's seen.
But I mean ships don't sink because of the water
around them, the sink because of the water
inside them and if that's not the best description
of what's wrong with our view of mental health,
then I don't know what is...
And if Keanu Reeves could find a way to clear
an impossible jump in a 19,000 pound vehicle
and Sandra Bullock could find it in her to
encourage him even though she knew of the
impossibility of this endeavor,
Then maybe, just maybe I can find a way to
make it through the night.
Maybe, if I try hard enough, I can sell myself the
idea that the bowling ball on my chest and the
albatross around my neck would look better on
display in a trophy case, my prized possessions a
reminder of my survival.
A reminder of my victory.
And maybe if I can find a way to keep my body
intact, to keep myself from splitting and needing
to replicate, to keep myself from bleeding dry or
opening up to let the water in then I can bear the
scars of previous attempts as medals, hanging

from my battered wrists, a reminder that I am
still alive.
And maybe if I can stay alive for one more
night, all of these awards and all of this
recognition will somehow find a way to be
shown to the world,
A retired athlete who is tired of running.
A retired boxer who is tired of fighting.
A retired veteran who is tired of killing, leaving
one more life for one more night.
And my bruised Knuckles
And scarred wrist
And that bowling ball
And that albatross
And that trophy case
And that shadow box of medals
And that broken down and beat up bus will be
enough to show somebody else that they are
capable of surviving to.
And in order to show someone else, I have to
first make it through tonight.
But hey, what is one more night?
One day at a time, right?

The Eulogy

Dearly beloved:

We are gathered here today to pay our final
tribute of respect to that which has been honored
by a long and vigorous life. Although met earlier
than expected and sometimes welcomed sooner
than the mortal flesh can ever understand, death
comes like a thief in the night and steals
everything that you're harboring away for our
protection. But this eulogy isn't low. No, you
have not been brought here for sad and
unfortunate mourning. In the words of Marc
Antony from William Shakespeare's Julius
Caesar, "I come to bury Caesar, not to praise
him. For the evil that men do lives after them
and the good is oft interred with their bones." So
here we are—to bury the evil and stop the
vicious cycle of abuse that you only see written
on bruised knuckles and scarred up arms.

The daily reflections of the Alcoholic's
Anonymous program says that "happiness nor
unhappiness is neither the point or the resolution
of our life". You see, beloved, far too often we
hear at these things that the departed was happy

and full of joy. We hear about all of the great things they did and all of the people that they impacted. But we never hear about the lies that they told or the hearts that they broke. We never talk about the bridges they burned, or the inventories they should have taken, or the amends that they could have made—and that my friends is why we are here today—to air out the dirty laundry that has been sitting at the bottom of the hamper for far too long. Let's take a moment to accurately lay to rest…

Me.

First off, let me preface this by saying that I am always right. If you ask anyone who has ever been in a room with me for more than about 5 minutes, they will tell you that I am always right—whether I am actually right or not. In A.A., they asked me if I wanted to be happy or I wanted to be right, and truth be told, I would rather spend 3 hours googling the Disney princess timeline than allow a 7-year-old to win an argument about animated movie lineage. So when I say these things, just know that I am always right.

You see—You're supposed to tell each other about all of my service work and charity—all of the trips that I took and the money that I donated. You're supposed to sit here and brag about the lives that I changed or my love of learning—as if it is any merit of yours that my grandfather read me Don Quixote while others snoozed to the 3 little pigs. You're supposed to laugh and cry as you tell funny stories about how I crashed my car through the fence at the bison reserve in Memphis when I was 17, or how I would dress up in a gladiator costume for football games at 18 after probably one-too-many Long Island Iced Teas. Maybe you'll mention the time that I tripped stepping up onto the curb while running and broke my wrist when I was 19. You're supposed to make jokes that end with phrases like "that's just how she was" or "she was always doing weird shit like that". You'll probably want to mention my love of pranks and how frustrated I get when I lose.

The point is that you probably won't mention that one specific word that we're all dancing around—one name given to me by my parents before me… not written across my birth certificate with pride but etched into my arms and my brain, worn like a red badge of courage

or a scarlet letter of shame. A name so vile that
it burns on my tongue, tracing rum trails down
my throat and into my veins, chasing the big
rush through my arms and legs to my brain
where it wages war against the dopamine that
has taken residence inside my head, pillaging
and plundering my happiness and leaving
nothing behind but a lengthy bar tab and one
killer ass hangover. We are talking about the
name that brought my mother and father to meet.
The name that drove our car to Vermont with my
stepfather and baby brother bundled next to me
in the seat. The name that left me in custody and
caused my grandfather to box up every memory
of my mother into a green plastic tote in the
right corner of the closet and behind reinforced
steel walls in his heart—until he could no longer
escape her face, my face, every time that another
candle was added to my birthday cake. We are
talking about the name that has kept me tap
dancing on the glass above my grave as I
choreographed my way through seizures in my
kitchen and hospital visits with I.V. drips. We are
talking about the name that stole my Elise, my
kindergarten best friend from us as she laid
alone in her room with a syringe in outstretched
arms, her body splayed out like a sacrifice,
nailed to the cross of her own sins, the same sins
seen by every street corner scum bag or foster

care drop-out. The same sins that left us sweating out or puking up words to stories told only in the movies or the young adult sections at bookstores that our parents would never tread. These are the names that are hushed at family gatherings, never spoken of and acted like they never existed— "Just take another Xanax mom, and act like it never happened."

It's the name that brought us all there, the darkened alley ways or bathroom floors where we believed that no one would find us—but the pile, the syringe, the bottle, the blade is a beacon, a homing device, an ashed out lighthouse, drawing us into the harbor of our own devices and leaving us shipwrecked along the shore of doubt and experimentation—We were motherfucking scientists on the verge of a breakthrough—adding chemical after chemical to try to find the perfect interaction to fix the imbalances in our brain—the imbalances in our lives.

No, you probably won't mention the name that drove me trap houses and bar bathrooms, that drove me to insanity, jay-walking time and time again and expecting something other than to be run down by life driving a steamroller. It's not really the kind of thing that we are taught to celebrate—our desire to self-destruct—to finally find the chemical compound to create the perfect atomic bomb. We were engineers—trying to win the arms race by finally giving up on our arms and settling for the vein in our legs instead. No, we are taught to only mention the good things—like our athleticism or our work ethic, but what if it was my devotion that kept me running to and from my desires. We are marathon athletes, continuing the race through the pain and the torture. What if it was the good in us that allowed us to disappear from your life—because let's face it, you were always better off without me anyways...

You see, Chris Angel and Harry Houdini don't have shit on me. They didn't have shit on Elise, or Chelsey, or Joel, or David, or Jared. No, those fakers didn't have shit on the man who stabbed my friend Austin, or my friend who just sank her relationship for a few milligrams of dope because she "simply needed to detox through the night." No, you see, illusionists manage to fool everyone around them while knowing the exact secrets of their trade. Us, we are left in the dark, fumbling for a lighter, a match in a river, drowning in our own minds, or in the dust that lines our maxed out credit cards—one last attempt to forget that we are the worst magicians alive—that we have only fooled ourselves into thinking that this is life.

But beloved, for all of the grief that this name has caused, I don't want you to hush it, or hide it, or silence it behind pleasantries or over exaggerated claims to my goodness—because the only reason why I stopped my truck on the way home for that drunk girl was because I remember what it's like to be the one left on street corners and bar stools, struggling with my spine to stay upright and struggling with my body to stay alive for one more night. No, it had nothing to do with me being a good person but was simply one more attempt to atone for the damage done in the name of escaping death as it clawed at the wooden doors of my life—taking a deep breath to huff, and puff, and blow down the houses that we all built around ourselves as we tried to blow the walls back out—I mean, isn't that what we were trying to do as we huffed, and puffed, and passed it all around?

For as ugly and pathetic as self-destruction can be, the phoenix can only be reborn once it burns itself to the ground and it's time that we reclaim this name and rise from the ashes, to stretch our wings and take flight—or whatever cliché shit you want to believe. It's time to break the chains that our weighing us down--- and blah blah blah—but the shame of this name is more like the bowling ball building in the throats of my family when they hear these words.

While at my funeral, you may poke fun at my fast driving or the way that I recklessly changed lanes, make sure to mention that I never found a reason to wear my seatbelt until I almost died. And while you may talk about how I enjoyed dressing up for parties and hosting events, make sure to talk about how I never knew what fun was until it was 3 am and I was completely sober in stitches, watching videos on youtube of people scaring each other. And remember that sometimes the bottle to your head and the bottle to your lips can be one in the same, my tongue acting as the twitchy finger ready to pull the trigger on my sobriety, on my life, sending parts of me across the room for someone else to pick up—just like every Saturday night before I walked into that room. And make sure to mention that even though I could talk your ear off, when I sat for too long or talked in front of people, or ever heard the phrase "hey, can I talk to you," I would pick at my fingers until they bled, trying to rip myself from my flesh or simply trying to silence the voices screaming in

my head that I'm not alright—and remember,
I'm always right.

When you sit down to write this eulogy, please
don't sugarcoat it or paint me like a masterpiece.
Show me for the 1st grade artwork that I am,
dripping glue at the ripped edges, stapled
together to sort of resemble a functioning
adult—if you tilt your head sideways and squint
your eyes a little.

Dearly beloved, I'm not asking you to be a dick,
but please be honest. I mean, I was only human
after all and it's really hard to write your own
eulogy once you're dead—So please be real…
but more than anything, use the name—the word
that makes them all cringe. Because maybe if
someone else would have told Elise that they
understood, she wouldn't have felt so alone.
Maybe if one more person, the right person, a
different person, would have reached out, she
could have found enough help, the right help,
different help.

So everyone take a deep breath and let's bury
this hatchet, or rather, drown the stigma under 6
feet of dirt and finally come out and say it…

I am an addict.

I may be in recovery. I may be clean and sober. I may be able to walk to the bar and order a rum and coke without the rum—and the bartender will say "so you just want… a coke?" and I can say "no bitch, I want a rum and coke but hold the coke… I mean the rum…. Shit…." I may have a chip in my hand and a clean breath in my lungs, but I am still an addict…

And sometimes just knowing that someone else is too is enough.

The Tremor

I awoke in a sweating tremor today in a heated house surrounded by warmth and wondering why the ice inside of my veins had not melted away. If everything outside of me was so calm, how could I continue to house a hurricane? You see, it's been 393 days since you passed. 393 days since you filled your blood with the dragon that coursed through our minds. 393 days since your body decided enough was enough. It's been 97 days since I picked up a bottle. 97 days since I last tried to drown a memory of who I once was. 97 days since I gave up the life that I lived and remembered that you… didn't… get… that… chance…

This morning I awoke with a tremor so bold that I shook the entire shoreline and created a tsunami that flooded over my brain, filling each crevice, each valley, each basin with doubt and anger. Why is it that I was able to walk away? Why was it that 97 days ago I was able to wake up and step out of my house and into a meeting when 393 days ago you continued to lie face down in the very same addictions that haunted me? Why is it that 97 days ago, I could exhale

the smoke from my lungs while you turned to
ash, each atom falling to the floor and blowing
away…

Blowing away like the smoke from our glowing
cigarette tips as we snuck around to the back of
my house, hiding from my grandparents with
our stolen cigarettes and 7th grade watered down
bottles of vodka—thinking we were the smartest
people around. Blowing away like the residue
inside our nostrils as we inhaled deep, choking
down the coughs as if it was our first time.

This morning I choked on my own words,
watching a bottle of liquor on my counter as if I
was waiting for it to move. I choked on your
name, a lump in my throat so large that even if I
did pick up the bottle, I would drown
immediately because there was no way in hell
that you were allowing me to swallow.

This morning I almost drown, but the funny
thing about drowning is that the swimmer,
unlike an alcoholic, knows that they're
drowning. Unlike the alcoholic, they're not
trying to swallow down their death—but that's
the problem. This morning I almost did. This
morning I almost drank, but your tremor

returned and reminded me, in a screaming tone, that

I

AM

ALIVE.

And that's a chance that you didn't get.

And even now, 97 days after I last picked up a drink, I sweat when I think about meeting our friends at a bar. Even now, 97 days sober, my mouth waters and my fingers shake and my mind races with the ideas of "just one drink" or "one more night won't hurt."

I wonder if that's what you thought. If 393 days ago you questioned if this was your last night. If you thought that was your last drink. If you thought you would wake up the next day, surrounded by warmth and love and life.

But you didn't

And I won't

And I have to wonder what you would think of me now. And what you would say. And how you would feel. And what you would be.

Because 393 days ago, addiction took a friend from me. And if I pick back up again, addiction will kill me.

To Thine Own Self Be True

To thine own self be true.

These are the words engraved on this blue chip that I anxiously flip between my fingers that have been popped one too many times through the fear of speaking in front of others.

To thine own self be true.

What the fuck is that supposed to mean?

I mean , how can I be true to myself if I don't ever know who that really is? I've spent so much time expertly crafting and aging this old craft wine of a facade of who I want you to see that I honestly forgot to ask the most important person if this was okay…

Me.

I mean, I guess that I'm a scholar. The $65,000 worth of student loans that I still owe to that bitch Sallie Mae and those 3 useless degrees that have never left those dumb cardboard tubes with that University of Tennessee sticker on them would seem to suggest that I'm educated. The plethora of trees killed for term papers and text books, my carbon footprint stomping a hole through my conscious as I spout words about conservation and global warming…. The list of writing assignments and article publications written between vodka shots and espresso shots might be enough to fool you into believing that I know what I'm talking about, but what good is a degree if I need a different degree, a different haircut, a different identity, a different sexual preference, or hell, even a dick to get a job around here…. Or at least the desire to sucking one and we all know that you couldn't pay me enough to sell myself to that system…. But that utility bill is due and as it turns out, toys r us will take you to court over a $200 past due credit card despite having declared bankruptcy and going out of business themselves and, I mean, if I'm going to get fucked either way, what's the point in fighting for my rights?

It's not like I own my uterus anyway.

It's not like my pussy isn't a preexisting condition just begging to be grabbed… I mean look at what I'm wearing? Doesn't this just scream asking for it?

And it's not like I can use that debt collection notice with the big red letters "PAST DUE " scribbled across the top to sop up my tears, or the leak in my living room ceiling, or the sweat of my rapist from my pillowcase as he returned to his fraternity house to paint the lion statue out front the color of my panties.

No.

I mean, I may be able to look at a bone and tell you the victim's approximate age, and sex-not gender because the two are actually different, you fuck bag… And I may be able to quote Hellenistic philosophy and clearly elaborate on Plato's allegory of the cave and how it is being fulfilled around us in daily life… And I may be able to clearly explain the inner workings of the 11 different identities of the 1970s dissociation case of Billy Milligan…

But those 6 years and 223 credit hours of undergrad never taught me to silence the pounding in my chest when someone texts me "Hey, we need to talk".

No, while they were too busy quizzing me on how the walls of the Roman Empire caved in, I was preoccupied fighting my own war-not with armor and swords but with the very breath in my lungs, beating at the walls that I rushed to support, plugging the holes in the levee and praying to stop the flood. With each breath making the walls of my chest paper thin, ripping and tearing, leaving a paper cut trail sketched out across my forearms like a white flag of surrender.

Just make it to September.

Just make it to September and you'll be another year older.

Another year wiser…

Another year smarter, and prettier, and thinner, and cleaner, and sober-er…

But September came and went and each year snuck in like a Trojan horse, disguised as adulthood and holy fucking shit….

You have no clue what you're doing…

And holy fucking shit…

You're still scared to death…

But you see, I was not bred to fear. No, I was born through adversity and lifted up by the scarred hands of a retired military cop and an overworked nurse, their knuckles callused by the slave wage spent to teach me to speak without a stutter. To learn to use my voice even when it falters and to speak through the tremors for those who can't and for those who don't have a voice . For those who have not yet risen from their ashes and those who know that today may be the day that burns them to the ground.

It's there that I learned to never give up trying.

Through the booming voices of speech pathologists who spoke through weirdly, 90s groomed beards that this little crack baby from the Memphis icu would never learn to process words or form sentences appropriately.

It's there that I learned to read.

While sounding out the words to Dante's Inferno and 20,000 Leagues Under the Sea. Lighting a fire under the asses and drowning out the claims of every middle aged case worked who said that they were too old to raise such a defiant child.

You see, where they saw defiance, she saw a broken promise and he saw his daughter-- another heart attack waiting to happen- long nights waiting for the smell of pot to come creeping through the windows that I conveniently left unlocked or an officer calling the home saying "we picked up her again R.W. you wanna come get her or do you want us to take her in?"

But he refused to sink and she was too stubborn to accept defeat and it was for this reason that I lived to see the day that they would place my grandfather into the grave, laying his fragile, broken heart to rest next to my grandmother's.

No, you see, my grandparents didn't raise a quitter and I guess that's why they got stuck with an addict, but hey, I'm still here so I guess that makes me a survivor as well…

As if the lines across my arms and the lines in my veins weren't enough to write you a novel on the definition of pain, let me break it down for you…

Most days I crave to die more than I want to be alive, but ultimately that decision isn't mine…

You see, I had this ugly cat that had the tooth
that stuck out of his mouth… And his other teeth
grew in around it and so then there were 2 that
stick out and he was so fucking ugly but so
fucking beautiful, but he would lick my hair if
no one had woken up to feed him by 730…

And I have this dopey dog that got hit by a car
when someone let her out of backyard and now
she walks with a limp, but that hasn't stopped
her from running to greet me when I come home
or jumping around when I pick up my hiking
backpack, knowing that she's going to be
coming with…

And I have this beautiful, kind, compassionate,
loving, generous woman who one day I may
very well call my wife…

And there's this girl who has never known a
home and is convinced that we are like everyone
else and that we are just going to give her back,
and that is why she ran, but all she wants is to
come home to a black light in her own room and
a shelf full of books, unpacked from the
backpack that she totes around no matter where
she goes…

And there's this feral blonde boy who looks just like me and is stuck with terrible dad jokes and awkward literary references as I stumble through this life of single motherhood and promise him that he will never know the pain of never feeling enough…

To thine own self be true.

I'm still not sure what that means or who that is, but I know exactly who I want to be and they say that progress occurs one day at a time… And I guess, as long as I'm waking up with the memory of an ugly cat licking my hair, and a weird dog smothering my face, my kids giggling in another room, and a missed text from someone way prettier than me, I'm doing okay.

And one day at a time, that's okay with me.

K.D.D.

Falling in love with you was the easiest decision of my life. Some days, it didn't even feel like a decision that I made on my own. Some days, it felt like it was something that happened to me. Like I was an active observer. Others, it was as simple as breathing, filling my body with life. It came so naturally. Like I didn't have to think. Like it was automatic. Like my body would continue to do it even if I didn't try. Like I'd die without it.

For you, it's not been the same. I knew this from the start. I watched as love brought weight to your heart, slowed you down and made you think—two things that you've avoided since you've been alive. "It's better this way," you would say, as you gathered my things in cardboard boxes and bags from our favorite stores. "I don't know how to be what you want from me." I could never tell you, but that was a lie. Simply being yourself has always been enough for me. Simply being mine would have been enough for me.

This house has never felt the same. The floor is cold and it hasn't been warm since you walked away from me that day. I've lit fires on my bridges just trying to stay warm, burning all of the letters and notes that I had left unsent- the top drawer of my dresser a mausoleum of my near unrequited love. The top drawer of my dresser the kindling for the blaze that was supposed to make me hate you. Hand-made flowers and ink on paper, folders full of photos, and plans scribbled on restaurant napkins—things that I kept in the off chance that you would change your mind and fall back into my arms like you had before. I wanted to be mad. I wanted to feel something different.

But it doesn't work out that way for people like me, does it? Because while you're still you, my heart will keep beating for sound of your voice.

Bowling Ball

Before I even met you I knew that I wanted you.

You added me on internet profiles and texting, because after all that's what millennials do, but I thought nothing of it. I mean, don't get me wrong, I stalked your pictures and videos and songs, because after all that's what millennials do, but I thought nothing of it.

I mean, you were cool- you are cool.

You were artsy- you are artsy.

You were perfect- you are perfect.

Why would I think anything less.

But I fell for your voice fast like a hurricane. Better yet, like a 16 pound bag of feathers falling off of Mt. Everest… or maybe it was more like a standard ten-pin bowling ball because it was anything but gentle. After all, they weigh the same… but when they crash down and hit rock bottom, which do you think will make a sound?

So I became a bowling ball for the first time in my life. And you told me things could be different. And oh are they different.

I may not be gay, but I know that in life the lines are not always black and white and sometimes it's a confusing sight to see a girl who intimidates the fuck out of me, but babe, you made it alright.

And I know that sometimes the shades aren't always primary colors, but speaking with you is always bright and watching you as you blow smoke rings into the air is like watching DaVinci working on the Mona Lisa or listening to Beethoven writing the 9th symphony…neither of them knew exactly what they were doing but it was perfect and it was pure. You're that last note in Beethoven's work- the one he would never hear, but the perfection that he would feel in his core. You're like an ocean wave as it crashes on to the sea, breaking and dissolving and bringing new life into me. But these words you'll probably never hear and this poem you'll probably never read, and in actuality that's alright because it's for the best- I wouldn't want to overwhelm you or anything like that- anything like I usually do.

And I understand that it's confusing- the fact
that after so much of life and so much of pain,
this is how we meet and this is how we play this
game? This is not the way that I wanted this
poem to go… so let me rewind
JJDGNJNSJDUAKMSTOAFVB there. We're
back at the start so we can start again and I can
listen to you speak as you speak softly to me.
But just know that before I ever met you, I
wanted you… and infatuation doesn't begin to
explain what I feel when your picture shows up
on my phone or your name in my inbox.

You're the fluttering in my heart and the sound
of air escaping my lungs as I debate whether or
not to pick up the phone. It's just flakiness I
know, but when there's potentially love
involved, it only hurts me more. Like rubbing
salt in the wounds or even better pouring
rubbing alcohol on the grazed knees of my
heart… But you understand pain and how to
heal that through art, and honestly that scares me
more than I thought.

I Was a Fallout

You found me on the cold bathroom floor. Surrounded by rich kids from the suburbs, I was the ultimate Trojan Horse, infiltrating their ranks and being welcomed in like I belonged. Like I was home. Home on a bathroom floor. And as they opened their doors, I opened my veins, allowing their world to flood my body, releasing the dragon into my bloodstream, allowing it to breathe its fire into me. He said it was his vices that drew the lines in my veins, mapping out track marks and cityscapes. It was his vices that were banging on the door to my brain, a splinter in my mind's eye, a Great Divide, ready to open up and swallow me whole. It was driving down an empty highway, late at night, with the red needle rising in my arms and in my dashboard. It was the tar burning in my lungs and beneath my tires. It was the crank of every gear in my engine and the chemical slowly filling my bloodstream.

It was the Fallout.

I was the Fallout.

My energy radiation dividing into four parts,
because that's how nuclear weapons work.
You see I was toxic.

40% blast. 50% thermal radiation. 5% ionizing
radiation. 5% residual radiation.

If you were there, you would probably be asking
"what the fuck are they saying?" But let me
break it down for you.

You see, first there's the explosion. This is called
the blast. This is where heat and radiation come
together and send a shockwave into the world
around me. This was the initial fall. This was
nights screaming and clawing at my doors,
watching as he pulled me back in, begging me
not to leave. This was times spent with my head
over a bowl, choking on the lies that I told and
throwing up the promises that I broke. This was
the stage of outward destruction, hail damage
across my forearms, the product of the perfect
storm that I had created.

Next comes thermal radiation. In any nuclear
detonation this makes up about half of the
energy released in the explosion. This is the
heat, the fires burning deep inside, igniting from
the tip of a burning out cigarette. These were the

lighters passed around on bathroom floors, pocketed from friends and lost through the holes in the bottom of grass stain denim pants. This was the bright red of stop lights that we refused to acknowledge, charging full speed ahead through the intersections, knowing exactly of the outcome, what kept us jaywalking through the streets at a snail and tortoise pace, not hesitating for the oncoming traffic whose lights radiated around us. This was the explosion that kept us warm as we trembled through another night alone, our minds screaming out "this is the last time" It's always the last time. "But no. This is actually the last time " And you literally say that every time. "I quit." "I give up" "I'm through" "I'm never going back."

Then there's ionizing radiation. These are the rays that make up only about 5% of the detonation but that hasn't stopped us from posting bright yellow and green warning signs on every radiation machine in hospital wards visited for every overdose, every panic attack, every stomach pump, every time that I heard the phrase "you have to eat." Or "did you even think?" These are the x-rays that saw straight through us, writing out our stories in transparencies, black and white, plain as day, a film illuminated by the fluorescent lights, buzzing like our insides. This was the outward manifestation of our inward chaos. Grinding teeth. Sinking cheeks. They say you can't see x-rays but they must have never seen the look on an addict's face when they finally get their fix. Because if you want to see what a real skeleton looks like, walk outside these doors and ask someone where to buy heroin. Because the skeletons we know aren't preserved in museums or proudly on display in research labs. No, they are walking among us, chasing the dragon around every sharp turn of tightly stretched collar bones and jaw lines sharp enough to slice cocaine lines, eyes sunk deep like the bottles we put to our lips every night, a trigger happy finger twitching around my neck, gripping tighter and tighter as if we were trying to choke out our own lives.

The last 5% is reserved for what's left over. This is the cleanup. This is the damage that you are left to see when you leave your storm bunker inside your brain, the safety that you've locked yourself away into, a dissociation case to rival the best, identities reserved for every human being that we meet. This is the residual. The waking up to a text message that says "we need to talk" or "I can't do this anymore" or "I thought I knew who you were"….

You see I never thought I was a nuclear bomb. I never thought that I was hell on earth. I never thought that I could be the source of the near-annihilation of the human species and what left civilization in ruins throughout the radiation washed globe.

But I mean, if I'm going to go out, I'm going to go big or go home and if being a ward of the court taught me anything it's to never get too attached to one place because you never know when you're going to have to leave. And if being a Trojan horse taught me anything it's to never assume that the words "I love you" mean anything.

But you see. That's where I fucked up.

You see, I got attached. And from the moment that I rolled my stupid fucking wooden horse through those gates and to the bathroom floor, offering myself as a sacrifice to the dragons at bay, I knew that I was fucked. And no matter how hard I fought. No matter how much I kicked and screamed and cried, no matter how hard I tried, I was trapped.

And in my heart I knew this to be true but in my head I still at war, a soldier in the front lines, pushing at the enemy gates as the powder turned liquid filled my veins.

But honestly, it only takes one missile to quash a rebellion and It only took one stray shot into a ventilation shaft to cripple the empire- and if you think about it, the fall of Rome literally happened overnight, even if every day before then led up to its demise.

And maybe I haven't hit my bottom. Maybe I haven't completely become the apocalypse. But just because I haven't gotten there yet doesn't mean that I won't. So I'll crawl out of this grave and don my hazmat suit and begin my relief efforts.

Because just because cleanup is long and just because cleanup is hard, that doesn't mean that it's impossible, and even if only one person survived the only 2 nuclear conflicts to ever occur, those odds are still enough to not give up on myself…

Even if you surrendered.

I'm Terrified You've Left Me

I'm exhausted of these road trips through
midnight--
Burning eyes, cheeks turn to red as knuckles
compress to white.
It's fucking cold outside and it kills me to think
of what I could have had
and all that I've wrecked with this bruised and
scarred hands.
I just want you here.
I just need you near.
Please, someone to tell me why
I can't seem to ignore these voices that lurk in
almost every night.
It's killing me inside.
They're killing me inside.
I keep drowning in the darkness in this cold.
I swear to god I'll never find my home
when there's nowhere else I want to go.
When midnight rolls around
I promise not to make a sound
because I'm scared that if I ask you to stay
that you'll turn and walk away.
Please don't walk away.
There were nights when this didn't feel quite so
permanent

but now it all feels like you'll get sick
of this or me and all of my consequence
and if I had to guess or project myself into
your thoughts for just a moment I'd say that I
wouldn't blame you
if you just said fuck it.
This brain space is absolutely cancerous,
ravaging my mind like the demons inside
that threaten to take me from this life,
but yet I fear
something more or less severe—
the words that make up my worst fears,
the ones that I'm terrified to hear.
I can't stand to feel this empty,
I'm terrified you've left me.

Her

You.

That is honestly all I need to write.

Because nothing more or nothing less will ever create something more beautiful than what god created that day.

You.